Madonna: Biography

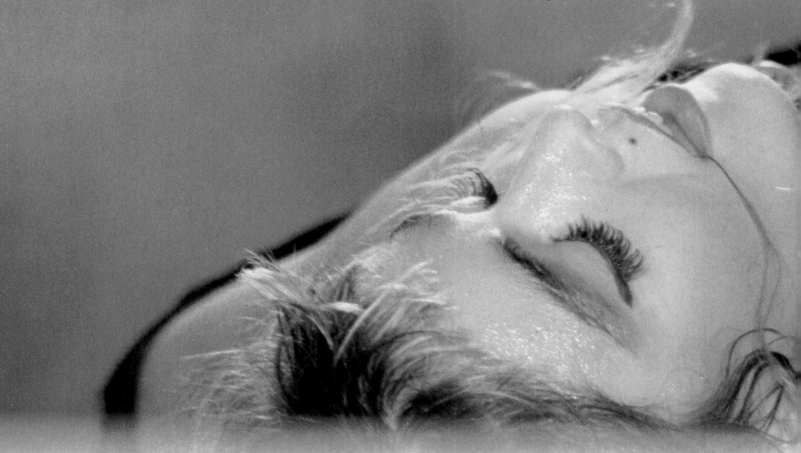

The saga of Madonna Louise Veronica Ciccone (No wonder she shortened it to, simply, 'Madonna'!), who was born August 16, 1957, or '58, or '59, depending upon your sources, is nearly unbelievable in its faithfulness to the classic American "rags to riches" success story. What makes it compelling, real and passionate, is the unique character of its central figure, Madonna.

Maybe it can be called a quirk of fate, the birth of this talented, strong, ambitious and beautiful girl into a large, traditional, Italian family, in Bay City, a suburb of Detroit, Michigan, during the heat of a new era, fuelled by an explosion called rock'n'roll.

From her family background, raised as she was in a competitive whirlwind of three brothers and four sisters, come some logical outgrowths in Madonna: her lively, outgoing personality, her non-stop motor-mouth, her insatiable capacity for fun times, her wry sense of humour, her need to conquer multiple challenges at once, and her unique sense of fashion, which seems to have come from a basic, make-do-but-be-different attitude. And her coming of age in Motown City, the virtual centre of life for soul and rock'n'roll music, must have had strong influences on her early predilection for dance, her insistence on a soulful, R&B-based musical direction, and her street-smart ways. Perhaps a very basic analysis, but one which keys into the roots of Madonna, who in fact is as highly complex and multi-faceted as she is talented and successful.

Little Nonni, as she was called in childhood, remembers a warm and loving home life up until the severe illness and death of her mother, for whom she is named. Madonna has beatific, tender memories of her namesake, and her eyes still well up with tears when she speaks of her. Also unforgettable for her is the depth of love her father had for her mother; it was into this void, in her mother's absence, that Madonna stepped as an eight-year-old, suddenly "the main female in the house, the one closest to my father."

A good student ("My father rewarded us with money for good grades, so I always got the best report card in the family"), Madonna soon assumed much of the

mothering role with her siblings: "I feel like all my adolescence was spent taking care of babies and changing diapers and baby-sitting. I have to say I resented it, because when everybody was out playing, I was stuck with all these adult responsibilities."

That resentment, however, gave birth to something important. A rebel by nature, Madonna was set on finding her way out of her Cinderella-like drudgery. And because she loved to dance, she convinced her father that, instead of taking piano lessons like her brothers and sisters, she should study ballet.

By the time she reached high school, Madonna was dancing consistently, spending up to five hours a day working out and taking lessons. She then won a scholarship to the University of Michigan, where she studied for five semesters under Christopher Flynn, who owned a ballet school in nearby Rochester. He became her mentor, encouraging her dedication and discipline.

She recalls, "I really loved him. He was like a brother and a friend, an imaginary lover, and my first taste of what I thought was an artistic person. He convinced me that I could do what I wanted to do, that I should go to New York and try for it."

True to form, Madonna saved enough money for a one-way 'plane ticket. In 1977 she landed in the city of her dreams, with $35 in her pocket and no place to stay. Relying for her survival on the generosity of strangers she met along the way, she eventually won a work-study scholarship at the prestigious Alvin Ailey Dance Theatre, where she danced briefly while holding a series of low-paying jobs in doughnut shops and fast-food joints, "jobs that I could never keep."

Next, she took a job as assistant to modern dance choreographer Pearl Lange. Madonna found her first apartment, "a roach-infested dump" on Fourth Street in the East Village, and liked it because "I knew it was the absolute worst neighbour-hood I could live in."

Soon enough, however, Madonna had changed course, zeroing in on music as her potential ticket to success. "I wanted to dance in New York, but all the good companies were full, they didn't need me. I couldn't wait five years to get a break, so I started going to musical theatre auditions." One of those auditions was for French disco singer Patrick Hernandez' international tour. The star's management smelled a good thing, and latched on to Madonna, taking her along to Paris and promising to make her "the next Edith Piaf."

Madonna recalls that "living in Paris was like a French movie. They introduced me to rich French boys that I hated. They'd take me to expensive restaurants, and I'd throw tantrums and refuse to eat, so they'd end up giving me money to make me happy. They dragged me around to show their friends what they had found in the gutters of New York. I felt miserable."

Six months later, she escaped by pretending she was going to New York for a visit. "But I left everything I had in Paris, and never returned." Back on her favoured turf, she joined a band called The Breakfast Club, and spent her days teaching herself to play instruments, and her nights with the band, playing all the Lower East Side dives, like Max's Kansas City and C.B.G.B.'s.

One night, Madonna tried singing lead, and actually won a lot of applause. When she wanted to repeat the experience, the band objected; eventually, this conflict broke The Breakfast Club apart. Madonna, never one to stand still, started her own band, called Emmy, after her nickname, affiliated with Gotham Management via Camille Barrone, a partner in the company, who began investing in her, paying for studio time for demo tapes. Eventually it became clear that the two had different concepts of Madonna as an artist; the manager saw rock, Madonna saw R&B.

Additionally, many pie-in-the-sky promises of large sums of money failed to materialise over time, although it does seem that Gotham made a healthy attempt to get a record deal for Madonna. The two parted, "not too amiably," and only met again in court several years later when Madonna was sued for breach of contract.

With this split, Emmy also broke up, although the band's drummer, Steve Bray,

stuck with Madonna. The two wrote songs, held sneaky late-night demo recording sessions in locked studios to which Steve often had keys, and generally lived a hand-to-mouth existence. Madonna says they ate for a dollar a day on a diet of peanuts and yogurt, sometimes found left-over food in rubbish bins, and often slept in rehearsal halls.

The next break came when Madonna used her feminine wiles to convince Mark Kamins, deejay at the Danceteria, an infamous, new wave, fashion zoo of a club in the Chelsea area, to play one of her tapes. Kamins obliged, and, as luck would have it, an A&R (talent discovery) man from Sire Records was present. Impressed with Madonna, he quickly channelled her to the label's president, Seymour Stein, who interviewed and signed her, on the spot, from his hospital bed.

Sire happened to be distributed by a major record label, Warner Bros. Madonna decided that it was time to have a major manager to go along with this deal. She thought, 'who is the biggest artist in the whole world? . . . Michael Jackson. His manager is going to be my manager.' She flew to Los Angeles, found her way to Freddy DeMann (who no longer manages Jackson), and, true to style, got exactly what she wanted.

Sire then released two 12″ singles, exploring public reaction to their new artist: "Everybody," and "Burning Up." Great dance-floor response and good sales led to the release of an eight-track début album, entitled simply, "Madonna." The album, spurred by the dance smashes "Holiday," "Borderline," and "Lucky Star," crossed over to the pop airwaves and has since sold over two million copies in the United States alone. Australia, England, South Africa, Germany, Holland and Japan quickly followed suit in consumer and media appreciation of the new craze called, simply, Madonna.

And the rest is history.

Madonna: History

In the short span of not-quite two years, Madonna rose from near-oblivion to become a media personality and superstar of the first magnitude. She has been called everything from "the Marilyn Monroe of the '80's" to "a trashy slut." Some critics talk about this 'phenomenon' as if she's committed a crime. So, herewith, for the rolls of history, is the incriminating evidence:

✻ Her début album, MADONNA, has sold over three million copies worldwide, and continues to sell.

✻ Her follow-up LIKE A VIRGIN, has sold nearly five million copies in the U.S. alone, and comes close to matching those sales internationally. At the peak of release, this LP was selling at the rate of 75,000 per day.

✻ She has had a string of top-ten singles from both albums, in the U.S. and internationally, while "Like A Virgin," "Borderline," and "Material Girl" all made it to No. 1 on the U.S. charts.

✻ The eight promotional videoclips she has generated have achieved the highest possible rotations and usage on TV in the world's major markets.

✻ Her début concert tour of the U.S. sold-out over 350,000 seats in record time. Merchandising sales on the tour have also broken records.

✻ She has appeared in three films:

A CERTAIN SACRIFICE
1984, by Cine Cine Productions, in which she stars. (An "underground" film, not yet in general release.)

VISION QUEST
1985, by Warner Bros. Pictures, in which Madonna does a cameo appearance as a nightclub singer.

DESPERATELY SEEKING SUSAN
1985, by Orion Pictures, in which she co-stars with Rosanna Arquette and portrays an eclectic, street-wise vamp. This film achieved the fifth highest U.S. box office gross; industry observers speculate that it was significantly fuelled by Madonna's rising star.

✻ She has established a clothing line, Yazoo, which is just starting distribution. Meanwhile, buyers for major stores report that their Madonna-inspired styles – from midriff shirts to lace gloves – are their hottest-selling items.

Madonna: A Day In The Life...

It is during the seventh song of Madonna's burning-hot concert that hundreds of large white balloons cascade from the arena ceiling, floating down like fat clouds into the outstretched arms of her clamouring fans. The balloons bear the phrase "Dreams Come True" in bold black type. It's a phrase that is probably the single most important key to the astounding success of the sexy blonde songstress/actress/comedienne. By her own admission, it speaks the philosophy that's brought her along the often-tricky pathway to stardom, international fame and wealth.

Fittingly, the balloons fall during the chorus of "Angel," a song Madonna wrote that epitomises a young girl's fantasy of a dream-boy-come-true:

You must be an angel
I can see it in your eyes
Full of wonder and surprise
And just now I realise . . .
Oooh, you're an angel
Oooh, you're an angel . . .
(Courtesy Warner Bros. Music)

Living up to her fans' hopes and dreams is the charge of the Virgin Tour, which is, in fact, the first ever in Madonna's young but explosive career. It began in Seattle, Washington, in April 1985, and crossed the U.S., delighting some 355,000 fans in twenty-seven cities (plus one in Canada) before reaching its sizzling finale in New York's Madison Square Garden in June. But Madonna's overseas fans may yet be satisfied, as the star will decide on the tour's possible international legs when she's finished baking "the big Apple."

Madonna, whose previous musical performance career consisted of dancing and singing a few songs live to backing tracks on the small stages of clubs like New York's Roxy and Paradise Garage, has admirably stood up to the pressures of a long tour.

She dances, prances and wriggles through a twelve-song set, often framed by her two attractive male dancers (boy toys?), Michael Perea, from New York City, and Lyndon B. Johnson (affectionately tagged "L.B."), from East Los Angeles. While she says, "I love to perform," Madonna admits that "life on the road is a gruelling and rough thing for me."

The voluptuous blonde star-on-tour awakes in the early morning to run, swim about one hundred laps, do aerobic exercises or work out on Nautilus machines, whenever the hotel has such facilities available. She then baths and dresses comfortably in her own Madonna-mode of fashion: often a tube skirt, work-out shirt, low-slung belt, fringed leather jacket, socks, deep-red patent-leather shoe-boots, hat and sunglasses, all topped off with a portion of her huge jewellery collection of crucifixes, rosaries, beads, bangles, bracelets and watches.

Dressed and ready to take on the world sans make-up, Madonna sometimes joins her manager, assistant and publicist for a light breakfast "meeting" of sorts; depending on the star's mood and energy-level, major decisions are achieved (add another song? dump the opening act?) . . . or left for later consideration. Together, they'll check out the previous night's reviews, which can be a ticklish issue since many critics have ragged the star in feverish, insulting tones that belie some deeply buried, possibly psychotic, jealousy.

Madonna, who is known for her cavalier ability to laugh off bad press, began to be somewhat sensitive mid-tour: "I get out

there and *work*. My fans love it, and they come from a wide age range, and all kinds of backgrounds. If they're happy, I'm happy – so much for all the goofs who wanna decide if my show deserves an 'R' or an 'X' rating . . ."

Her publicist reminds Madonna that the newspaper in question is likely to receive 2,000 angry phone calls from her ardent fans that day. Madonna agrees, shrugs it off, jokes with the hovering waitress, and zips off to a waiting limousine to be whisked away to the airport.

Her mood is characteristic of her own unique version of "life in the fast lane": nothing stops her; if it gets her down it won't be for long; no grass grows under her feet; for every 'no' there are at least five 'yes's' waiting in the wings. She leaves last night behind her, moving on to the next city, the next show, new fans and new reviews.

In flight, Madonna's likely to prop her legs up on the first-class seat in front of her, make a few remarks to her also-blonde-also-a-dancer assistant Annie, and doze off until the plane lands. Meanwhile, across the aisle, her 6' 8," 280-pound Afro-American security guard keeps a watchful eye on his blonde charge.

Nearby, Madonna's manager goes over

the books, checking over merchandising and
ticket sales and planning the schedule for the
coming night. The twenty-eight city sold-out
tour is estimated to have grossed over $6
million, and has broken merchandising sales
records ever since the fifth date in San
Francisco.

Special rush orders for cut-off "Boy Toy"
sweatshirts, lace-trimmed midriff tops and
eight other styles of shirts, crucifix earrings,
plastic and rubber neon-coloured bracelets,
pendants and rosaries, buttons, posters and
tour books, had to be filled at a moment's
notice by the merchandising company, who'd
mistakenly thought that the Jackson's
"Victory" tour merchandising was the largest
they'd ever handle in this musical era.

Beyond the clear demand for concert
tickets and all the Madonna-things, this tour
is a lucrative one because, true to the star's
personality, it handles luxury with reason as
opposed to greed.

They travel on commercial, not private
planes; they bus for short distances; they
don't have blow-the-roof-off parties every
night; they use three equipment trucking
rigs (Prince's Purple Rain tour had thirteen)
and a modest-but-skilled crew of thirty-six.

On arrival, Madonna is the leader of the
pack, much as she is the real director-
behind-the-scenes of the whole tour. (She
has final approval on *everything*.) Stepping
along the airport corridors in her hat and
sunglasses, she might make it through
without drawing a crowd, unless L.B., with
his infamous huge beat box (the classical-
trained keyboardists in the band have
hatched more than one plan for bombing the
box and saving their eardrums), which must
weigh forty pounds and booms relentless
decibels of rap and street-funk music,
catches up to her, inspiring Madonna to cut
loose in a series of breakin' moves and dance
steps near the American Airlines exit.

Outside, while her British tour manager
checks details on the various limousines and
vans, counting heads and checking on the
hand-carried instruments, Madonna
continues to boogie, laughing and cutting up
with her companions. "I'm soooo hungry,"
she exclaims, "who's got food?" L.B. produces
a small plastic bag of sunflower seeds,
assorted nuts and dried fruits. "Great,"
Madonna says, taking a first munch as her
tour manager comes along to hustle her into
the waiting silver stretch limousine, with its
obligatory colour TV and stereo radio/
cassette system.

At the hotel, Madonna is swiftly shown
to her suite, where Annie instantly unpacks
the star's personal essentials. Madonna
appreciatively sniffs the scents of several
floral arrangements, samples some fruit in a
gift basket, eyes a still-frosty gift magnum of
champagne ("Ugh . . . not now . . . headache
city"), reads the cards attached to the

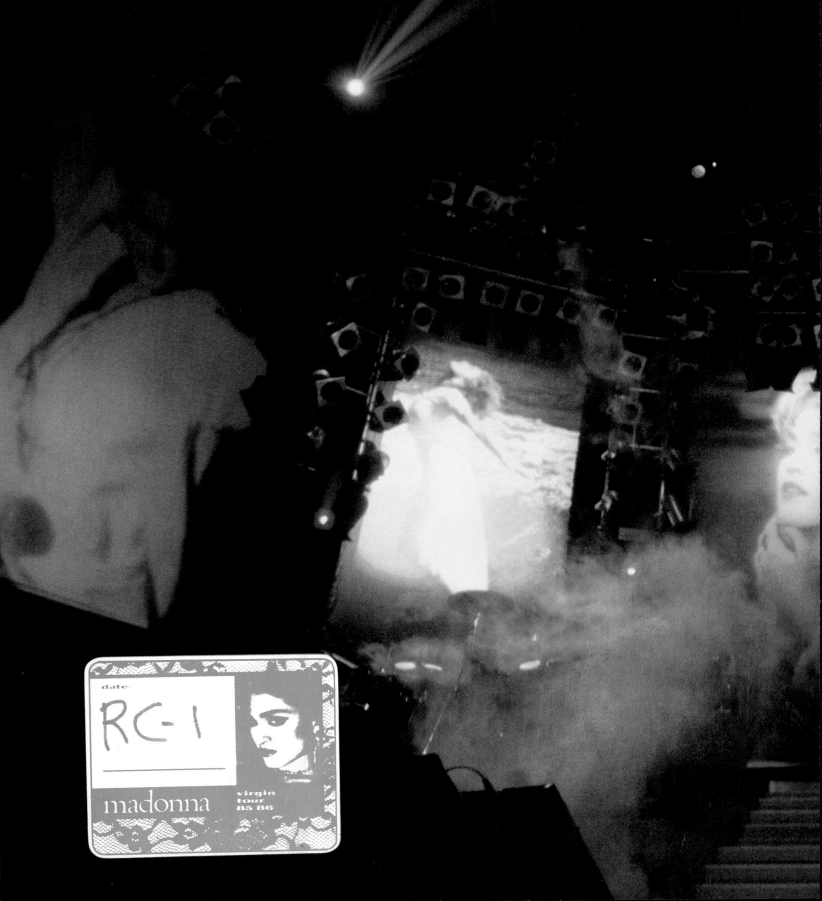

Madonna: Vi

gin Tour 85/86

various presents, glances at some telegrams and messages, and then heads either to the telephone or to the bed for a nap.

Downstairs, the remainder of the tour party checks in; the bellmen hurriedly deliver over one hundred pieces of luggage to the rooms, and everyone disperses for the two-hour break before the appointed meeting time to travel to that night's venue.

Meanwhile the road crew, driving from the previous night's show, have arrived at the arena and begun setting up for the concert.

Madonna's younger brother, Christopher (tall, lean, brown-haired, blue-eyed and handsome), who's in charge of her on-stage wardrobe along with those of the dancers and band, shows up and begins organising things for later transfer to a small tent on the rear of the stage, where Madonna will make three quick changes during her set.

Now she arrives with her manager, who accompanies her to her dressing room and sees that everything's okay before joining the tour manager, accountant and promoter to go over final details. In some cities, the ceilings and walls of Madonna's dressing room have been completely covered with pink and silver balloons; others have offered

lavish floral arrangements trimmed with ribbons and lace.

Madonna now has a choice: relax, listening to her portable radio or the latest series of new cassettes brought by a friend who flew in for last night's gig; have a rare manicure; swap jokes with Annie and Christopher; complete the lyrics for a new song that's been in progress for a week; or view and approve some of the latest colour slides of her performing, one of which will soon be used for the cover of a big American magazine. She takes a stab at the slides, but after a series of groans, shoves the lot back into the chrome case and heads for the telephone.

She rings up Rosanna Arquette, her co-star in the film, DESPERATELY SEEKING SUSAN, and they trade stories on the latest happenings. Rosanna hears Madonna relate how Prince called that afternoon and said he really missed her; how she couldn't sleep the night before because she missed her regular long after-show telephone love-in with boyfriend/actor Sean Penn, who was shooting night scenes for his new movie on location in Tennessee.

While the two star-friends talk, Madonnna's band are organising themselves for a local TV-news interview. Of the thousands of interviews requested of her, Madonna has granted only four during the course of her tour.

She has said that the no-interview syndrome is not a function of ego or nasty superstar inaccessibility, but rather involves "my need for a little privacy and a lot of fun! Honestly, I did loads of interviews when my first album was heating up. Of course, some people didn't *want* to talk to me then. But, those who did, who had a sense, or an intuition, that I was headed somewhere, all got some of my time. But now it's become something I don't really enjoy any more . . . it's work, and it can be boring, 'cause I do get tired of answering the same questions over and over."

By now, the backstage pace is fast and furious, with last-minute sound-checking and adjustments, caterers setting up food for the band and crew, a video director meeting with Madonna's manager to discuss their latest project, and local TV crews and photographers filing in to claim their pre-arranged credentials and receive their instructions for that night's work.

Annie bolts out of Madonna's dressing room and asks a female caterer the location of the nearest store where expensive make-up can be bought. Annie races down the corridor and disappears through the stage door; she has only thirty minutes to run the errand before Madonna begins her cosmetic artistry for the show. While she does, from time to time, use a makeup artist, Madonna prefers to do her own face: "I know it better than anybody does!" The star also does her own hair, even cutting it herself (witness the recent addition of short bangs).

Suddenly, it's show-time. At 7:25 p.m., the fans had begun to enter the arena, like a stream of Madonna look-alike contestants (or Madonnaquins), paying homage to their idol with gloves, rag-tied heads, beads, bangles, layered net shirts, bare midriffs, cut-off lace tights, neon-painted fingernails and countless other carefully detailed accessories.

At 8:00 p.m., The Beastie Boys opened to mixed reactions (a third of the way through the tour, the harsh criticism lodged against the Beasties inspired Madonna to sneak into the audience to personally evaluate their show; she came away more resolved than ever to keep them on as openers). At 9:00 p.m., following an intermission during which the Madonnaquins, ranging in age from seven to twenty-five, have literally purchased tons of merchandise, the arena lights go down and the fans shriek with anticipation.

Glamour shots of Madonna are projected on to five huge screens that hang behind the band. The synthesizers start the sizzling intro to "Dress You Up." Madonna's silhouette appears on the centre screen in material-girl/Statue of Liberty stance, and holds stock-still just long enough for the crowd to reach fever-pitch. The screen rises, and a beaming Madonna joins her two dancers in a provocative arm-in-arm walk down the rear-centre-stage stairs.

Aglow with the joy of performing and the warmth of the crowd's acceptance, she dances, skips, hops, slides and stomps her way through the opener and the next two numbers, "Holiday," the pop-dance smash that put her solidly on the world music map, and "Into the Groove," the infectious upbeat single from the DESPERATELY SEEKING SUSAN movie.

For these three hip-popping numbers, Madonna's attire is neon-colourful: a blue-green knit mini-skirt, waistband rolled down to reveal the top of her purple lace cut-off tights and her world-renowned belly button; a blue-green lace midriff top, which goes with the motion to show a purple lace brassiere; a pink, spiked, hip-riding belt; short black spikey-heeled boots; purple lace fingerless gloves; a bright, tailored multi-coloured woven jacket in hues of orange, yellow, white, purple, green and black. She also wears a purple bow-rag in her hair, a large gold cross earring and necklace, joined by a few long strands of beads, and a silver peace symbol hanging from a leather string. ("My favourite crucifix is real big and chunky . . . actually, it's a piece of art, but I can't wear it on stage, 'cause it's so heavy it might swing up and hit me in the head.")

Racing offstage to change after the third number, Madonna is paced by the aggressive playing of her tight-knit, six-man band, who exercise some bassy-but-fiery jazz-rock riffs until the star re-appears atop a great riser on stage left, heatedly gyrating to the opening chords of "The Gambler," a tune she penned and performed for the film VISION QUEST.

Now she's all in black: cat-lady sunglasses; sleeveless, body-tight, midriff-baring shirt with a cross, bordered with shimmering black bugle beads, cut out of the fabric just above her cleavage; skin-tight black leggings that end three inches above her punky spiked black boots; a fringed mini-skirt with matching fringed over-the-elbow gloves and a bugle-beaded vest patterned in crosses. It's a hot outfit, and a hot Madonna who dances frenetically, grinding suggestively, thrusting her pelvis toward a strategically-placed pole on the riser.

Finally, she vaults fifteen feet down on to the stage, falls and lays there, stretched out and breathing hard. She, and the fans, savour the moment. Madonna rises on one elbow and sings the first lyrics to "Borderline." She flings away the glasses and sheds the vest;

23

KEITH HARING AND
LARRY LEVAN INVITE YOU TO THE PARTY
OF LIFE AT 84 KING STREET. 9 P.M. TILL?
MUSIC BY LARRY LEVAN AND JUAN DUBOSE @
ART AND VIDEO BY KEITH HARING INFO. 4062080
FREE ADMISSION WITH THIS INVITE ADMIT 2

K. Haring
84

MAY 16 PARADISE
1984 at GARAGE

24

down to her bare-black essentials, she then delivers the silky ballad "Crazy for You," another No. 1 U.S. single, from the VISION QUEST soundtrack.

Next comes "Angel," balloons and all, and "Over and Over," which ends symbolically as the blonde powder-keg and her two dancers pose in a dramatic triangle beneath a huge peace sign. Now comes the show's inferno, "Burning Up," which, like the video before it, plays well on the jilted lover/faithless woman theme, culminating in the rise of a virtual bank of hazy smoke, as Madonna goes to her knees in front of her handsome guitarist, James.

The lights remain dim, and a silent interlude affords the stunned audience a chance to recover and demand an encore. The wicked sexpot of the last song returns as the virgin bride in white, teasingly asking the crowd, "Will you marry me?" As they scream "YES!!" Madonna again takes the

stage, now in an '80's-camp wedding dress, swathed in countless yards of sheer white veil that wafts around her lace-and-rhinestone, brief tuxedo jacket and hip-hugging skirt that flares out in prima-ballerina layers of tulle before ending at the knee.

Complete with fingerless white lace gloves and sleek, short white boots, Madonna's wedding gear moves beguilingly as she cruises the stage, faithfully rendering "Like A Virgin," her septuple-platinum album's title song that hugged America's No. 1 spot for seven solid weeks. Midway through the song, the surprised crowd screams its approval as a few bars from "Beat It," complete with Michaelesque dance steps, form an instrumental bridge.

The show closes with "Material Girl," which matched "Like A Virgin" chart-wise. Madonna is carried on stage by three he-men. Twirling yards of gleaming white pearls, and clad in high-glamour white sequinned tube skirt and strapless top, she is delicately set down on stage, and swaddled in a white ermine stole. "You don't *really* think I'm a material girl, do ya?" she teases. As the audience resoundingly replies, "YEAH!" Madonna reaches into her top and pulls out wads of – MADONNA MONEY – flinging it into the crowd, saying, "take the money, it's caused me nothin' but trouble!"

She polishes off the song with high energy; when she exits the stage, her fur is forgotten, hanging on a mike stand. The crowd hears a deep, stern, male voice offstage: "Madonna, get off that stage now!" She replies, still offstage, in her best little-girl voice, "But Daddy, do I have to? I'm having *so* much fun . ." Daddy barks again, "Get off *this instant,* do you hear me, young lady?" Madonna, material girl to the world, retorts, "Oh, all right, but at least let me get my *fur.*" She races back onstage to thunderous acclaim, throws the crowd a kiss, and disappears into the night.

In Detroit, at Madonna's hometown show, her real Dad, Sylvio "Tony" Ciccone, actually appeared on stage to drag his wilful daughter off. Not only the audience, but incredulous newscasters, came away telling tales of "A startling family rift that ended the show." Meanwhile, having the last laugh, Madonna confides, "I kept telling Daddy how important it was to make the whole thing look real. I guess he got the point, 'cause the first time we did the act, he almost pulled my arm out of the socket!"

Madonna: Quotes

"All those men I stepped all over to get to the top, every one of them would take me back because they still love me and I still love them."

"Art and music can never be too permissive especially if they act as an alternative to the reactionary attitudes of people like Reagan and the Moral Majority."

"From when I was very young, I just knew that being a girl and being charming in a feminine sort of way could get me a lot of things, and I milked it for everything I could."

"I wanted to do everything everybody told me I couldn't ever do."

"Losing my virginity? I thought of it as a career move" (big laugh).

"Madonna is my real name. It means a lot of things. It means virgin, mother, mother of earth, someone who is very pure and innocent but someone who's very strong."

"When I was growing up, I was religious in a passionate, adolescent way. Jesus Christ was like a movie star, my favourite idol of all."

"I come from a large Italian American family in Detroit. I had a very strict Catholic upbringing. My father never approved of me staying out or dating boys. He never wanted me to be a dancer or singer because he came to America poor and lived in a Pittsburgh ghetto. He wanted me to study law, not to do anything flakey. Now he's seen me on TV and in magazines he's quite proud of me, though he doesn't approve of it at all."

"I live in a huge loft – 2000 square feet – in Soho, Lower Manhattan. It's where all the artists are. Talking Head David Byrne is a neighbour. My loft space has bare floors, windows on every wall, a bed, a table and chairs. That's it. Oh no . . . I have lots of mirrors for my choreography. New York's very *street*, busier than London. I eat in Little Italy and always have spudini, an appetiser. It's delicious and fattening."

"Popcorn is about my favourite food in the world. It cleans your system, it fills you up, and it's cheap."

"Prince is a friend of mine. But the first time we met, he called me 'ma'am'."

"I considered getting married once but it seems like a silly idea now for me, not people in general. I can't conceive of living happily ever after or happiness for a long period of time with one person. I change so much and so my needs change too."

Discography

Videography

ALBUMS

MADONNA
(Sire Records 1-23867)
Released in July, 1983.
"This album is dedicated to my father."

(Side One) "Lucky Star," written by Madonna, produced by Reggie Lucas, engineered by Jim Dougherty; "Borderline," written and produced by Reggie Lucas, engineered by Jim Dougherty; "Burning Up," written by Madonna, produced by Reggie Lucas, engineered by Jim Dougherty; "I Know It," written by Madonna, produced by Reggie Lucas, engineered by Jim Dougherty.

(Side Two) "Holiday," written by Curtis Hudson and Lisa Stevens, produced by John Jellybean Benitez, engineered by Michael Hutchinson, mixing engineering by Jay Mark; "Think of Me," written by Madonna, produced by Reggie Lucas, engineered by Jim Dougherty; "Physical Attraction," written and produced by Reggie Lucas, engineered by Jim Dougherty; "Everybody," written by Madonna, produced by Mark Kamins, engineered by Butch Jones.

LIKE A VIRGIN
(Sire Records 1-25157)
Released in November, 1984.
"This album is dedicated to the virgins of the world."

(Side One) "Material Girl," written by Peter Brown and Robert Rans, produced by Nile Rodgers, engineered by Jason Corsaro with Rob Eaton; "Angel," written by Madonna and Steve Bray, produced by Nile Rodgers, engineered by Jason Corsaro with Rob Eaton; "Like A Virgin," written by Billy Steinberg and Tom Kelly, produced by Nile Rodgers, engineered by Jason Corsaro with Rob Eaton; "Over and Over," written by Madonna and Steve Bray, produced by Nile Rodgers, engineered by Jason Corsaro with Rob Eaton; "Love Don't Live Here Anymore," written by Miles Gregory, produced by Nile Rodgers, engineered by Jason Corsaro with Rob Eaton.

(Side Two) "Dress You Up," written by Peggy Stanziale and Andrea LaRusso, produced by Nile Rodgers, engineered by Jason Corsaro with Rob Eaton; "Shoo-Be-Doo," written by Madonna, produced by Nile Rodgers, engineered by Jason Corsaro with Rob Eaton; "Pretender," written by Madonna and Steve Bray, produced by Nile Rodgers, engineered by Jason Corsaro with Rob Eaton; "Stay," written by Madonna and Steve Bray, produced by Nile Rodgers, engineered by Jason Corsaro with Rob Eaton.

Madonna also appears on these albums:

WOTUPSKI!?! by John Jellybean Benitez
(EMI America Records MLP-19011)
Released in May, 1984.

(Side One, Track Two) "Sidewalk Talk," performed by Jellybean with Madonna, written by Madonna, produced by Jellybean.

REVENGE OF THE KILLER B'S, VOL. 2
(Warner Bros. Records 1-25068)
Released in October, 1984.

(Side Two, Track Five) "Ain't No Big Deal," performed by Madonna, written by Steve Bray, produced by Reggie Lucas, engineered by Jim Dougherty.

VISION QUEST ORIGINAL MOTION PICTURE SOUNDTRACK
(Geffen Records GHS 24063)
Released in February, 1985.

(Side One, Track Four) "Gambler," performed by Madonna, written by Madonna, produced by John Jellybean Benitez, arranged by Steve Bray.

(Side Two, Track Five) "Crazy For You," performed by Madonna, written by John Bettis and Jon Lind, produced by John Jellybean Benitez, arranged by Rob Mounsey.

SINGLES

EVERYBODY
Sire Records, 1982.

BURNING UP
Sire Records, 1983.

HOLIDAY
Sire Records, 1983.

BORDERLINE
Sire Records, 1984.

LUCKY STAR
Sire Records, 1984.

LIKE A VIRGIN
Sire Records, 1984.

MATERIAL GIRL
Sire Records, 1985.

DRESS YOU UP
Sire Records, 1985.

ANGEL/INTO THE GROOVE
Sire Records, 1985.
12" only.

CRAZY FOR YOU
Geffen Records, 1985.

EVERYBODY
(1982) Madonna's first promotional video, filmed in performance at New York City's Paradise Garage.

BURNING UP
(1983) Producer, Simon Fields for Limelight Productions; director, Steve Baron; cinematographer, King Baggot; art director, Julie Towery; stylist, Maripol.

BORDERLINE
(1984) Producers, Bruce Logan and Michele Ferrone for Bruce Logan, Inc.; director, Mary Lambert; cinematographer, Andrea Dietrich; art director, Simon Maskell.

LUCKY STAR
(1984) Producer, Glenn Goodwin for Faultline Films; director, Arthur Pierson; cinematographer, Wayne Isham; art director, Madonna; music re-mixer, John Jellybean Benitez.

LIKE A VIRGIN
(1984) Producer, Simon Fields for Limelight Productions; director, Mary Lambert; cinematographer, Peter Sinclair; art director, John Ebden; stylist, Maripol.

MATERIAL GIRL
(1985) Producer, Simon Fields for Limelight Productions; director, Mary Lambert; cinematographer, Peter Sinclair.

GAMBLER
(1985).
CRAZY FOR YOU
(1985).
Both clips are comprised of footage taken from the film VISION QUEST, in which Madonna appears as a night club singer.

INTO THE GROOVE
(1985) Comprised of footage from the film DESPERATELY SEEKING SUSAN, in which Madonna co-stars.

Note: "Burning Up," "Borderline," "Lucky Star," and "Like A Virgin" are available on the commercial videocassette, "Madonna" (Warner Music Video 38101-3).

"Money's not important. I never think I want to make millions and millions of dollars but I don't want to have to worry about it. The more money you have the more problems you have. I went from making no money to making comparatively a lot and all I've had is problems. Life was simpler when I had no money, when I just barely survived."

"I swim 100 laps every day just to keep in shape. It's good to have a supple body, you can move around a lot more easily and it's a lot more visually appealing."

"I really learnt to dance on my own. I watched television a lot and I used to try to copy Shirley Temple when I was a little girl. I used to turn on the record player and dance in the basement by myself and give dance lessons to my girlfriends in my five-year-old manner. As I got older I started giving lessons to boys too, and I remember the first guy I gave lessons to . . . the song was 'Honky Tonk Woman' by The Stones. When I was about twelve I decided I should try to get pro about this and started going to the schools where they teach jazz, tap, baton twirling and gymnastics. It was just a place to send hyperactive girls."

"I had to do everything on my own and it was hard to convince people that I was worth a record deal. After that I had the problem of convincing the record company that I had more to offer than a one-off girl singer. Warner Brothers is a hierarchy of old men and it was a chauvinistic environment to be working in because I was treated like this sexy little girl. I had to prove them wrong, which has meant not only proving myself to my fans but to my record company as well. That is something that happens when you're a girl. It wouldn't have happened to Michael Jackson or Prince."

"Boy George makes me sick."

"I'm getting tired of being compared to Marilyn Monroe. I still wear lots of jewellery, but I'm tired of wearing all that stuff as well, because Cyndi Lauper's doing it now. What I'm doing now is letting my hair grow out. And it's going back to its natural colour, which is actually dark. But I think I'm still going to look pretty wild and eclectic."

31

Madonna: What The Stars Foretell

Madonna's sun falls in Leo, the sign of royalty, self-confidence and creativity. This placement is the ultimate indication of natural star quality. Leos are born performers, and Madonna's magnetism and playful sense of drama are Leo traits shared by other natives of this sign – like Mick Jagger.

Leo's are attention-getters because the sun is most at home in this zodiacal position. Madonna has the irresistible dazzle and queenly flair of this sign, and since it's also the sign of the heart, she is warm, outgoing and naturally optimistic.

Uranus – the planet that rules individuality and daring – falls conjunct her Leo sun, an indication that she is strong-willed, highly intuitive and something of a rebel. This conjunction is the harbinger of a meteoric rise – giving her unstoppable energy, a powerful sense of self, and a compulsion to break free from restrictions and act from her real feelings.

Madonna's moon is in Capricorn, an earthy, disciplined sign which shows that her success is the result not only of inborn talent – but hard work. Capricorn is an ambitious, practical sign and the moon in this position adds to her drive, indicating that she sets impeccably high standards for herself – and doesn't compromise.

In Madonna's chart, Venus, the planet of love, is in almost exact conjunction with Mars, the planet of energy and aggression – a combination that imbues natural sex appeal. And it's interesting that these two planets fall in the sign Virgo (the virgin) – considering both the choice of her name and the words to one of her hottest hits. Venus and Mars in Virgo indicate that despite the fact that she projects a sexy image – Madonna is highly discriminating in her choice of men – and though she can act wild, her true nature is quite refined.

Mercury conjunct her natal uranus indicates that Madonna is unusually quick, intelligent and creative. Neptune squaring mercury shows that she can be quite dreamy, and has an inborn flair for music, as well as a streak of psychic savvy.

Jupiter in Scorpio is an indication that Madonna has very strong feelings, loves the good things of life and has a rich sense of humour. Saturn in Capricorn adds to her determination to succeed, and since this planet trines pluto in Virgo, she has the ability to transform difficult situations into winners.

Looking at Madonna's upcoming aspects, it seems as if she'll continue to enjoy more and more success for a long time to come. After her birthday in 1985, there may be new dimensions in her career with an emphasis on her creativity and an expansion of her focus. She will receive a huge amount of publicity and will be the subject of countless interviews and headlines. In the late winter of 1986, she'll be faced with an important decision of the heart which will affect her through November 1987. And it looks as if she'll want to stay free for a while to come – since it's the spring of 1988 that brings her the kind of emotional bliss everyone dreams about.

Grace Lytton